SOMETHING
Good
IS TRYING TO
HAPPEN TO YOU

SOMETHING *Good* IS TRYING TO HAPPEN TO YOU

MAJOR JOHN R. CHEYDLEUR, PH.D.

THOMAS NELSON
Since 1798

NASHVILLE DALLAS MEXICO CITY RIO DE JANEIRO BEIJING

Published in Nashville, Tennessee, by Thomas Nelson. Thomas Nelson is a trademark of Thomas Nelson, Inc.

Thomas Nelson, Inc., titles may be purchased in bulk for educational, business, fund-raising, or sales promotional use. For information, please e-mail SpecialMarkets@ThomasNelson.com.

Unless otherwise noted, Scripture quotations used in this book are from:
The Holy Bible, New King James Version. © 1982 by Thomas Nelson, Inc.

Library of Congress Cataloging-in-Publication Data
Cheydleur, John R.
  Something good is trying to happen to you! / John R. Cheydleur.
    p. cm.
  ISBN 978-1-4041-1393-0 (pbk. : alk. paper)
  1. God (Christianity)—Goodness. 2. Providence and government of God—Christianity.
  3. Encouragement—Religious aspects—Christianity. 4. Consolation. I. Title.

BT137.C44 2009
231'.8—dc22

2009008004
Printed in the United States of America
09 10 11 12 13 DP 6 5 4 3 2 1

DEDICATED TO

My children,
Amy, Jim, and Andrew,

My graduate students
at the Alliance Graduate School of Counseling,

And my Cadet students
at The Salvation Army School for Officer Training

What Can You Do When Nothing Works?

Sometimes you just feel "busted and disgusted."
Nothing seems to be going right; everything seems to be going wrong.
You have no new thoughts. No inspiration from anywhere.
Everyone around you seems negative.
The skies are gray, and the weather is your least favorite temperature.
The bank account is approaching zero.

What can you do when nothing works?
Open up this book.
Something *good* is trying to happen to you!

Dear Friend,

Let's not pretend. When bad things are happening to you, they are bad, not good.

However, the biblical story of Job teaches that though the bad things in your life are real . . . they are not sent to you by God. The Bible also teaches that even while bad things are happening, good things are also trying to happen to you.

The message of this book is that you can reach up your small, trembling hand and place it in the great, good, and mighty hand of God.

You can learn how to cooperate with God for your benefit.

Something good *is* trying to happen to *you*.

Major John R. Cheydleur, Ph.D.
West Nyack, New York

INTRODUCTION

Congratulations! Your good future starts today.

Two Positions

You are in one of two good positions in life: either you are currently receiving generations of blessings from the faith of your ancestors, or you can begin initiating generations of blessings for those who will follow you.

Either way, your faith is important, and it will be rewarded. Your every action, deed, and decision is important to make your life better too.

Something good is always trying to happen to you. Will you block the good or allow yourself to receive it?

*J*ess Lair was a hard-driving Minneapolis advertising executive who collapsed with a heart attack in an elevator. From this position, which at first seemed so negative, he renounced selfishness, found God, and rebuilt his life by going back to school and earning a Ph.D. in psychology.

His first book, *I Ain't Much, Baby—But I'm All I've Got*, was a runaway bestseller.

Jess experienced far more success depending on God than he had ever found in his former, self-driven life.

> *"What then shall we say to these things? If God is for us, who can be against us?"*—Romans 8:31

RECOGNIZING A "GOD-CIDENT"

You may ask, "If something good is always trying to happen to me, how can I know it?"

You can learn to recognize when a "God-cident" comes into your life. A "God-cident" is different from an ordinary "incident" or a mere "coincidence."

DEFINING THE DIFFERENCE

An "incident" is a minor event in which you perceive no particular meaning.

A "coincidence" occurs when two or more seemingly connected events happen in such a way that you sense meaning, even if you can't define it.

A "God-cident" is an unexpected intervention by God. It is meant for your good.

You can still believe something good
is trying to happen to you even when
you can't see God's hand.

*M*ary made minimum wage cleaning office buildings at night to take care of herself and her son. One week she ran out of food three days before payday and had only enough money saved to pay the rent on her apartment. She tried to borrow some money from a coworker, but he didn't have any extra to lend her.

Unsure whether to buy food or pay the rent, she turned to her Bible. After reading it, she decided she should pay the landlord on time and trust God for the food. So she got into her old Chevy, which had no air conditioning, and drove with the windows down to the rental office.

On the ride home, a fifty-dollar bill blew into her car and landed on the dashboard. Grateful for God's goodness, she thanked Him and drove directly to the supermarket and bought enough food to last her and her son until payday.

AVOIDING WHAT IS TRYING TO HARM YOU

Even as a new Christian you have an old "garbage monster" dredging your past for sludge that can be thrown in your face.

As the oldest enemy of humanity, Satan will attack your mind with punishing thoughts and ungodly fantasies that threaten to choke off your newfound faith, intent on doing whatever he can to discourage and defeat you with negativity.

Anytime such thoughts begin to creep in, turn them over to Jesus as soon as possible.

You might be hesitating to do good or to receive good because you have done something bad or failed at something in the past.

Confess that old sin or failure to Jesus, and move boldly into the good future God has prepared for you.

> *"If we confess our sins, He is faithful and just*
> *to forgive us our sins and to cleanse us from all*
> *unrighteousness."*—1 John 1:9

DON'T . . .

listen to your "garbage monster."
   Squish its ugly head back into the pile and tell it to shut its mouth.

DON'T . . .

listen to anyone, even Christians, who try to keep you down. They are your "drag-you-down" people.

You know who they are, and you can see them coming. They minimize your successes, making your major triumphs seem small and the little grace notes of your life seem unimportant.

Stay away from them as much as possible.

> *"Trust in the LORD with all your heart, and lean not on your own understanding; in all your ways acknowledge Him, and He shall direct your paths."*—Proverbs 3:5–6

Of course, bad things can happen to good people. Yet even then, God is able to change your outcomes from bad to good.

Do . . .

Look at some of the negative traits from your past and ask God to turn them into positive traits for your future.

> "Delight yourself also in the LORD, and He shall give you the desires of your heart. Commit your way to the Lord, trust also in Him, and He shall bring it to pass."—Psalm 37:4–5

Do . . .

remember that no matter how sinful or emotionally crippled your past was, something good is trying to happen to you—not only in your future, but right now! Look for it!

In your past you might not have had enough family stability, discipline, or unconditional love. If that is the case, find some mature older people in your church who can be your support system and help you in your weakest areas.

They are your "cheer-you-on" people. They will help you to become a steadfast Christian. They will also applaud you for your successes, grieve with you at your failures, and want the best for you all the time.

A pull-up from a "cheer-you-on" person is not the same thing as a put-down from a "drag-you-down" person.

> *"Let all bitterness, wrath, anger, clamor,*
> *and evil speaking be put away from you,*
> *with all malice. And be kind to one another,*
> *tenderhearted, forgiving one another, even*
> *as God in Christ forgave you."*
> —Ephesians 4:31–32

FACE YOUR FEELINGS

You may be disappointed at your own past failures or angry at the sins of others against you. Such feelings create an emotional burden that blocks you from receiving the good God has for you.

As much as possible, you have to give all your sins, burdens, and resentments to Jesus so that you're ready to receive the something good He has waiting for you.

> *"Therefore humble yourselves under the mighty hand of God, that He may exalt you in due time, casting all your care upon Him, for He cares for you."*—1 Peter 5:6–7

$\mathcal{B}$ob was devastated when his "garbage monster" blew the whistle on one of his shameful secrets in a public meeting. It turns out that Bob had dropped out of high school and was still cursed with the distorted image of himself as a drop-out . . . even though he had gone back to school and obtained his GED . . . even though he had completed two full years of college courses at a good community college . . . even though he had held successful ministry and social services positions in several communities and had received the applause of community leaders.

"Drop-out" was Bob's "garbage monster" label. It hurt him every time he thought about it, even though it was no longer true.

Since that wake-up call of a meeting when Bob realized the damage his "garbage monster" was doing, Bob has worked to overcome the negativity with the help of God and his good wife. Not only is his public persona that of a success, but in the core of his being Bob knows that God has helped him rebuild his life and his self-image.

Yes, the old "garbage monster" label still pops up sometimes, but now Bob knows that good things are happening to him every day. And that's where he puts his focus.

Building Up Your Personality Strengths

There are three layers to your personality:

Your public layer

Your emotional layer

Your core beliefs layer

Your core beliefs layer is the most important. Always believe in Jesus Christ and follow His teachings.

YOUR THREE PERSONALITY LAYERS

Public Personality	*Surface Presentation* Your chosen face to the world. Includes planned behaviors.	Subject to learning, reading, and thinking.
Emotional Personality	*Reactive Self* Your face that shows when you are under pressure.	Responds to music, art, and love.
Core Personality	*Deep Beliefs and Values* Your secret face before God. This is your resource pool and guide for life.	Engaged by Christian experiences and Scripture.

Build up your public layer

    by reading the Bible to learn right actions.

Build up your emotional layer

    with good Christian music, art, and uplifting media.

Build up your core beliefs layer

    by fellowshipping with older Christians who know how to pray

    and by praying yourself.

RECEIVING THE GOOD

God is always sending you the good. Your ability to receive the good increases as each layer of your personality is turned more fully over to Him.

> *"For I know the thoughts that I think toward you, says the LORD, thoughts of peace and not of evil, to give you a future and a hope. Then you will call upon Me, and . . . I will listen to you. And you will seek Me and find Me, when you search for Me with all your heart."*—Jeremiah 29:11–13

Remember, your "cheer-you-on" people are your encouragers. They are God's resources for the development of your renewed personality. Seek them out.

> *"Be kindly affectionate to one another with brotherly love, in honor giving preference to one another."*—Romans 12:10

GIFTED

Romans 12:6–8 says that we are each given different personalities and spiritual gifts: "Having then gifts differing according to the grace that is given to us, let us use them: if prophecy, let us prophesy in proportion to our faith; or ministry, let us use it in our ministering; he who teaches, in teaching; he who exhorts, in exhortation; he who gives, with liberality; he who leads, with diligence; he who shows mercy, with cheerfulness."

Idea: Choose one gift from the above list that seems to fit you the best. Practice this gift as often as you can.

YOUR GUIDING PRINCIPLE

Develop a guiding principle that matches your own God-given personality and that allows God to bless you for who you are. Don't pretend to be someone you are not.

*C*arol is a divorced mother raising four children by herself. Some women would be overwhelmed by such circumstances, but Carol has discovered a guiding principle that complements her personality and economizes her time.

That guiding principle is to tell the truth as soon as possible, even when it is awkward or inconvenient.

Carol never settles for a vague answer when an honest answer can be given. As a result, everyone trusts what she says. And because her "yes" means yes, and her "no" means no, she doesn't have to waste time and energy making up new stories for new situations.

Carol's commitment to be true to her core personality—and to her personal sense of God's purpose for her life—enables her to be a consistent mother, a professional teacher with strong integrity, a trustworthy friend, and a dependable church volunteer.

MAKING BETTER DECISIONS

There are five levels of increasingly God-oriented decisions that will promote the most good for you and those you love.

LEVEL ONE:

Gut-level, God-oriented Decisions

These are "leap of faith" choices that propel you toward God.

Because gut-level decisions tend to be somewhat emotional, they need to be stabilized at one of the four higher levels when possible.

"For by grace you have been saved through faith, and that not of yourselves; it is the gift of God, not of works, lest anyone should boast."—Ephesians 2:8–9

LEVEL TWO:

Personally Beneficial, God-oriented Decisions

These involve making choices to do the right thing while knowing the right thing also results in more good for you. Such decisions recognize that people are actually better off in this life, as well as the next, when they follow Jesus.

Of course, without a firm God-orientation, any decision made just for personal benefit can descend into selfishness. Such a decision would at best be of short-term value to yourself or anyone else.

> "I am the vine, you are the branches, He who abides in Me . . . bears much fruit; for without Me you can do nothing."—John 15:5

LEVEL THREE:

Rightly Relating, God-oriented Decisions

When you make these kinds of choices, you are doing the "love your neighbor" thing that Jesus taught us to do, whether it helps you or not. At this third level, our Christian decisions go beyond our own direct benefit to benefiting others.

This outward-looking approach helps you strengthen your own faith commitment. Of course many non-Christians also help others. But as a Christian, you will be of more help to those around you than you were as a non-believer.

"He who walks with wise men will be wise, but the companion of fools will be destroyed."—Proverbs 13:20

LEVEL FOUR:

Rules-based, God-oriented Decisions

These decisions involve making the right choice just because the Bible says so, even when you don't understand it. When you make such a decision, you are trusting God to know more than you know.

Since He is wiser than you are, first follow God's Word; then ask for His help to understand.

"My son, if you receive my words, and treasure my commands within you, so that you incline your ear to wisdom, and apply your heart to understanding; yes, if you cry out for discernment, and lift up your voice for understanding, if you seek her as silver, and search for her as for hidden treasures; then you will understand the fear of the LORD, and find the knowledge of God."—Proverbs 2:1–5

LEVEL FIVE:

Spiritually based, God-oriented Decisions

At this level you are doing the right thing, with the faith that it is the best thing for everyone. You may not have a specific rule or Scripture that tells you exactly what to do. The choice comes from an internalized Christianity powered by the Holy Spirit. It is the mature expression of your growing faith.

> *"When He, the Spirit of truth, has come, He will guide you into all truth; for He will not speak on His own authority, but whatever He hears He will speak; and He will tell you things to come. He will glorify Me, for He will take of what is Mine and declare it to you."*—John 16:13–14

LOVE-BASED DECISIONS

When in doubt, love your friend, love your enemy, love yourself.

You will find that more and more good things are happening to you.

> *"This is My commandment, that you love one another as I have loved you. Greater love has no one than this, than to lay down one's life for his friends."*—John 15:12–13

*J*im played Little League baseball in San Diego with future golf legend Phil Mickelson. Even though Phil's dad had a personal passion for golf, he made a level-three family decision to help Phil in his baseball experience, so he bought a pitching machine.

Then Mr. Mickelson decided to help all the boys on the team and meticulously taught each of them how to hit well.

While he had decided to become a Little League coach for his own son's benefit, Mr. Mickelson also served for the good of all the team members.

Today, Jim is all grown up and teaching his own son to surf the Pacific's waves. He still remembers that it was Phil's dad who showed every boy on that San Diego Little League team that he was capable of becoming a winner in any endeavor.

RISING TO HIGHER STANDARDS

When seeking the right decision,
use the Scriptures as your higher
standard.

GREAT OLD TESTAMENT STANDARDS

Start with the Ten Commandments. They are found in the book of Exodus, chapter 20.

These rules have formed a foundation for successful decision-making for thousands of years:

1. *"I am the Lord your God . . . You shall have no other gods . . ." (vv. 2–3).* This means get rid of any Ouija™ board, rabbit's foot, lucky coin, horoscope, pentagram, or pyramid. Also, eliminate any basis for decision-making that puts other spiritual practices on the same level with, or above, the worship of God. It will save you a lot of trouble and keep you a lot more sane.

2. *"You shall not make for yourself a carved image. . . .*
You shall not bow down to them nor serve them" (vv.
4–5). This is not about innocent lawn sculptures;
this is about false, man-made gods that mess up your
decision-making enough to hurt your family for
three or four generations. Do not risk the fate of your
great-grandchildren on any "garbage gods."

3. *"You shall not take the name of the LORD your God in vain"* (v. 7). If you want to demean yourself by being rude and crude, leave God's name out of it. No decision to make here at all. Just don't do it.

4. *"Remember the Sabbath day, to keep it holy"* (v. 8).
   Verse 9 goes on to say, "Six days you shall labor and
   do all your work, but the seventh day is the Sabbath
   of the LORD your God. In it you shall do no work."
   (And neither should your family or your
   employees—look it up!)

   God built our physical bodies to operate best
   when they get weekly rest. If your employer
   makes you work on Sundays, you will still be
   better off if you find one day a week to put your

feet up and reflect on God and life and how it all fits together. This instruction not only prevents workaholism but also the greedy exploitation of people.

5. *"Honor your father and your mother"* (v. 12). This commandment further tells us that good family relationships promote longer lives for all concerned. The stress of painful or neglected relationships hurts everybody. (It wouldn't kill you to send your mom or dad a birthday card, would it?)

6. *"You shall not murder"* (v. 13). Okay, so somebody did you wrong. Let God—or the state—deal with them, but don't decide to do it yourself. You were not meant to be judge, jury, and executioner.

7. *"You shall not commit adultery"* (v. 14). It's easy to discern the right decision here: no sex with anyone who is married to anyone else. Stay sexually faithful to your own marriage, no matter how good-looking the other person is or how unhappy she or he claims to be. If you're not married, wait. Wait. Wait. Single is single. Married is married. You can't be both at the same time.

8. *"You shall not steal"* (v. 15). Not even one grape or one pencil. If you are sure your boss wants you to permanently take home that computer, ask him to confirm it, preferably in writing.

9. *"You shall not bear false witness against your neighbor"* (v. 16). Car accidents? Personal injury claims? Sometimes it's okay to seek what's yours; just don't lie about the other person. It will come back to haunt you.

10. *"You shall not covet your neighbor's house"* (v. 17)—
or wife, husband, butler, maid, sports car, SUV, or
anything else. Work hard and obtain the things you
need for you and your family. Then you can still be
friends with the folks next door.

For additional guidelines in the Old Testament, look at
Isaiah, chapter 58, for information about the benefits of
freeing people from oppression.

HELPFUL NEW TESTAMENT GUIDELINES

The book of Ephesians, chapter 6, lists a powerful arsenal of faith weapons, which Scripture refers to as "the whole armor of God." You as a believer can now decide to use these tactics instead of the less effective (and sinful) tactics of the past that harmed others and attacked your self-respect.

THE ARMOR OF GOD

Using these new weapons will build your self-respect.
They are:
- the Belt of Truth, instead of lying;
- the Armored Vest of Right Living, instead of an evil lifestyle;
- the Shield of Faith, instead of pessimism;
- the Helmet of Salvation, instead of a damned future;
- the Sword of the Spirit, not the false spirit of drugs and alcohol;
- the Word of God, not evil fables and get-rich-quick TV offers;
- praying always, instead of worrying often;
- being watchful and steady, instead of neglecting your duty and making excuses;
- speaking boldly for the Gospel, instead of being a tongue-tied coward.

—Ephesians 6:12–19

LIFELONG VALUES

See chapters 5 and 6 in Ephesians for some New Testament guidelines regarding a stable family life.

In order to have stable self-confidence and gain the respect of others, you will want to develop your own self-respect first. Start with the Lord.

> *"The LORD is your keeper; the LORD is your*
> *shade at your right hand. The sun shall not strike*
> *you by day, nor the moon by night. The LORD*
> *shall preserve you from all evil; He shall preserve*
> *your soul. The LORD shall preserve your going*
> *out and your coming in from this time forth, and*
> *even forevermore."—Psalm 121:5–8*

See Galatians 5:19–21 for a list of
things to decide against, and then
consult verses 22 and 23 for a list of
virtues to develop so that something
good may more easily happen to you.

r. Will personally developed and directs a fine social work program at a leading Christian college. He is a very successful person, even though his public persona is that of a pessimist.

How can this be?

Dr. Will shrewdly uses his strategic realism to get others to stand up against him and present optimistic alternatives. And he has a secret: nothing can make Dr. Will quit, run away, or even slow down when he believes he is working toward a worthy goal.

When you break through Dr. Will's exterior, you find a determined bulldog who can't be intimidated because he chooses each academic project to match the highest Scriptural standards. This above all enables him to really believe in what he is doing.

USING SCRIPTURE DAILY

On March 6, 1941—well before America entered World War II—U.S. President Franklin D. Roosevelt ordered that a New Testament be given to every Protestant soldier training for battle.

The United States of America joined the war against Hitler nine months later, almost to the day: on December 7, 1941. President Roosevelt recognized how important it is to have a copy of Scripture with you at all times.

GET YOUR OWN, CARRY YOUR OWN

To help you receive the most good, carry a Bible or New Testament with you in your pocket, purse, backpack, or briefcase, and read it in your spare moments. Also, look up special Scriptures that others share with you.

If you don't have a Bible to call your own, ask your pastor or local Christian bookseller to help you obtain a pocket- or purse-sized copy of the Scriptures. If there is a Salvation Army nearby, seek out your local Corps Officer for a free copy of The Salvation Army's *Personal Faith New Testament*.

Don't let poor heredity or bad circumstances keep you down. Instead, begin to memorize inspirational Scriptures so your faith can boost you to new heights.

HERE ARE TWO GOOD STARTERS:

"Be strong and of good courage; do not be afraid, nor be dismayed, for the Lord your God is with you wherever you go."—Joshua 1:9

"Those who wait on the Lord shall renew their strength; they shall mount up with wings like eagles, they shall run and not be weary, they shall walk and not faint."—Isaiah 40:31

CONFRONT YOUR DOUBTS

Deliberately confront and replace any doubts you have with affirming Scriptures from your New Testament. Write down the passages you most want to remember, or enter them into your computer.

> *"If any of you lacks wisdom, let him ask of God, who gives to all liberally and without reproach, and it will be given to him. But let him ask in faith, with no doubting, for he who doubts is like a wave of the sea driven and tossed by the wind."*—James 1:5–6

Remember, it is God's forgiveness, God's love, and God's presence that always brings you the financial help, emotional healing, or physical strength you need. His Word will point you to those truths each day.

> *"Bless the LORD, O my soul; and all that is within me, bless His holy name! Bless the LORD, O my soul, and forget not all His benefits: who forgives all your iniquities, who heals all your diseases, who redeems your life from destruction, who crowns you with lovingkindness and tender mercies, who satisfies your mouth with good things, so that your youth is renewed like the eagle's."*—Psalm 103:1–5

STRIVE FOR BALANCE

Don't get overextended with your church work. Save time for God, for prayer, and for meditating on the Scriptures. And stay connected to your family with times of good, clean fun.

> *"Come to Me, all you who labor and are heavy laden, and I will give you rest. Take My yoke upon you and learn from Me, for I am gentle and lowly in heart, and you will find rest for your souls. For My yoke is easy and My burden is light."*—Matthew 11:28–30

LISTEN & CHOOSE

Listen to the voice of God by reading Scripture in your own quiet time.

Also, as you hear sermons and read your Bible, write down or underline the verses that touch your heart. Read over each one of these personal "heart Scriptures" for twenty-one days, so that they sink deep into your soul.

One of the best verses for new or recommitted Christians to take to heart is: "Let this mind be in you which was also in Christ Jesus" (Philippians 2:5). Let this be your spiritual goal.

A great Scripture to memorize is: "No weapon formed against you shall prosper" (Isaiah 54:17). This is one of God's many promises to you. It will help you combat anxiety.

Martin Luther, the founder of the
Lutheran church, had a favorite
Scripture verse. It was Romans 1:17:
"The just shall live by faith."

YOUR LEGAL BLESSINGS

There is a great list of God's blessings in the Old Testament book of Deuteronomy. The first thirteen verses of chapter 28 reveal the good things that God wants to give his people.

You are allowed to pray for all of these things. But pray for obedience most of all.

"Now it shall come to pass, if you diligently obey the voice of the LORD your God, to observe carefully all His commandments which I command you today, that the LORD your God will set you high above all nations of the earth. And all these blessings shall come upon you and overtake you, because you obey the voice of the LORD your God."—Deuteronomy 28:1–2

"Blessed shall you be in the city, and blessed shall you be in the country.

"Blessed shall be the fruit of your body, the produce of your ground and the increase of your herds, the increase of your cattle and the offspring of your flocks.

"Blessed shall be your basket and your kneading bowl.

"Blessed shall you be when you come in, and blessed shall you be when you go out."—Deuteronomy 28:3–6

"The LORD will cause your enemies who rise against you to be defeated before your face; they shall come out against you one way and flee before you seven ways.

"The LORD will command the blessing on you in your storehouses and in all to which you set your hand, and He will bless you in the land which the LORD your God is giving you."—
Deuteronomy 28:7–8

"The LORD will establish you as a holy people to Himself, just as He has sworn to you, if you keep the commandments of the LORD your God and walk in His ways. Then all peoples of the earth shall see that you are called by the name of the LORD, and they shall be afraid of you.

And the LORD will grant you plenty of goods, in the fruit of your body, in the increase of your livestock, and in the produce of your ground, in the land of which the LORD swore to you our fathers to give you."—Deuteronomy 28:9–11

*"The LORD will open to you His good treasure,
the heavens, to give the rain to your land in its
season, and to bless all the work of your hand.
You shall lend to many nations, but you shall not
borrow. And the LORD will make you the head
and not the tail; you shall be above only, and not
be beneath, if you heed the commandments of
the LORD your God, which I command you
today, and are careful to observe them."*
—Deuteronomy 28:12–13

Colonel Lyell Rader of The Salvation Army was known for the "No Bible–No Breakfast and No Bible–No Bed" pledge cards he distributed.

His purpose was to get people to focus on Scripture both at the beginning and end of their days in order to sharpen their ability to hear the voice of God and to make godly life decisions.

KNOWING GOD'S WILL

Some people say you cannot know God's will for your life.

It's true that there are some things we cannot know in advance. Yet God has clearly expressed His will—what He desires from us—in the following six directives, which are all drawn from Scripture. These are just a few examples of God expressing His will in His Word.

◇ Love God with a pure heart.
◇ Be joyful as often as you can.
◇ Do not have sex outside of marriage.
◇ Enjoy sex inside your marriage.
◇ Pray regularly.
◇ Always give thanks for something.

"For this is the will of God, your sanctification: that you should abstain from sexual immorality; that each of you should know how to possess his own vessel in sanctification and honor."—1 Thessalonians 4:3–4

"Rejoice always, pray without ceasing, in everything give thanks; for this is the will of God in Christ Jesus for you."—1 Thessalonians 5:16–18

Jesus' Two Greatest Commandments

Matthew 22:37–39—

> *"Love the Lord your God with all your heart, all your soul, and all your mind."*

> *"Love your neighbor as yourself."*

*A*teenager who was in one of Dr. Tom Harris's *I'm O.K.—You're O.K.* therapy groups told the story of standing on a street corner while the light was red. The boy's inner parent was saying, "Don't cross." His inner child, on the other hand, was saying, "Go ahead, step on out." And while he was debating about what to do, the light turned green.

We would be so much better off if we gave up any false sense of urgency, took the time to think things through, and made the best decision rather than automatically opting for the quickest one.

Sometimes, the good thing God is sending us is a green light. If we just wait for His action, we may not have to struggle with a decision after all.

Something good is trying to happen to you. Don't block it with an impatient choice.

GOOD THINGS FOR A LIFETIME

In order to have good things happen to you consistently throughout your lifetime, you will want to create balanced goals in these four important areas of life:

◇ Physical health
◇ Social relationships
◇ Spiritual growth
◇ Financial stability

NEWS FOR YOUR FUTURE

There are two completely different kinds of natural factors that strongly affect your future.

Consider these "Good News" and "Bad News" factors when you are planning for good health, positive relationships, spiritual growth, and financial stability.

The five natural "Good News" factors that will help your health, relationships, spiritual growth, and financial stability are:

1. Work you like to do

2. Responsibilities

3. Recognition

4. Achievement

5. Advancement

These factors make it easier for you to keep receiving good things from God.

On the other hand, the five natural "Bad News" factors that can make you most dissatisfied and even harm your health, relationships, spiritual growth, or financial stability are:

1. Negative physical or social environment

2. Insufficient income

3. Unsatisfying personal relationships

4. Culture of negativity

5. Poor supervision

These factors may even tempt you to resent God, or to become so disappointed in Him that you stop expecting good things from God.

Robert was a supervisor for a California telephone company when it downsized. He had to take the buyout they offered him or risk losing his retirement.

His dream was to help Christian camps, schools, and churches with the construction and the repair work which they needed, but could not afford.

To begin, Robert started a handyman business in his town. He liked the work, but did not have group support. Later, he helped a group that was trying to invent an electric car. There was a supportive environment, but they paid him nothing. Robert never surrendered his dream.

Today, he and his wife travel the western states in their motor home, working with a Christian construction group that repairs and revitalizes ministry properties at little or no cost.

Like Robert, your life goals can come true.

Balancing Your Goals

In order for good things to happen to you all throughout your life, you need a balanced plan so that your goals support each other.

In the next several pages you will be able to create four useful charts to help you balance your goals. Each of the four life areas—physical health, social relationships, spiritual growth, and financial stability—has three pages: a Helps Page, a Sample Page, and a blank My Page for you to fill in your own goals.

Let's begin!

Before you chart your goals:

◇ Think about whether there will be enough possible "Good News" factors and few enough of the "Bad News" factors to realize your goals.

◇ Talk to God and a trusted friend or pastor to help you decide what can work for you. If you need to make any adjustments to your dreams or plans, do so now.

◇ Consider whether you will need to change your personal relationships, job, or social environment to receive the good things you need from God. If so, make a note to yourself in the margin of your chart.

MY FIVE-YEAR PHYSICAL HEALTH GOALS
HELPS PAGE

5 Years   The first question to answer on your Physical Health chart is: "What do I want to be able to do physically five years from now?"

3 Years   Now look at the five-year Physical Health goal you created. Ask yourself, "What could I be doing physically, in three years, to move toward my five-year goal?"

1 Year   Next write a definite step—accomplishable in one year—that supports your three- and five-year goals.

6 Months What activity that you can do in the next six months would help you toward your long-term goals?

2 Weeks Name something here that's easy to do soon, and that doesn't require money or anybody else's cooperation, so that there is a strong opportunity for your success.

MY FIVE-YEAR PHYSICAL HEALTH GOALS
SAMPLE PAGE

5 Years *Run a half marathon in my city.*

3 Years *Run two miles daily.*

1 Year *Run thirty minutes daily.*

6 Months *Jog thirty minutes, three times a week.*

2 Weeks *Look at running shoes in shoe store.*

MY FIVE YEAR PHYSICAL HEALTH GOALS
My Page

5 Years _____

3 Years _____

1 Year _____

6 Months _____

2 Weeks _____

MY FIVE-YEAR SOCIAL
RELATIONSHIPS GOALS
HELPS PAGE

5 Years   Pray for God's insight as you fill in your five-year Social Relationships goal. Make it something that is really important to you.

3 Years   Ask yourself, "What do I need to be doing in three years that will assure me that I am on the right track to reach my five-year goal?"

1 Year   Name one or more concrete activities you can do with the person or people you named in your five-year goal.

6 Months Ask yourself, "What can I be doing six months from now that is directly related to my five-year Social Relationships goal?"

2 Weeks Choose something simple you can try out to prepare for a better or stronger relationship. Count it as a success when you do it, independent of the other person's response.

MY FIVE-YEAR SOCIAL
RELATIONSHIPS GOALS
SAMPLE PAGE

5 Years   *Have a strong, loving relationship with my wife and children.*

3 Years   *Sponsor my children's clubs or sports activities monthly. Share a date night with my wife.*

1 Year   *Teach each of my two sons a new sport or activity. Take a second honeymoon to Hawaii with my wife.*

6 Months *Host three family/neighborhood barbeques next summer, with games for children.*

2 Weeks *Select a nightly bedtime story to read to my children. Ask my wife to choose one TV show for us to watch and discuss together.*

MY FIVE-YEAR SOCIAL
RELATIONSHIPS GOALS
My Page

5 Years _____

3 Years _____

1 Year _____

6 Months _____

2 Weeks _____

MY FIVE-YEAR SPIRITUAL GROWTH GOALS
HELPS PAGE

5 Years   Ask yourself, "What could I be doing in five years to have a more spiritually adventurous lifestyle?"

3 Years   Name a specific activity here that will show you that you are well on the way to your five-year Spiritual Growth goal.

1 Year   Ask, "What can I build on from my six-month goals?"

6 Months Ask yourself, "What changes can I make in my prayer life, Bible study, or other spiritual activities that point me toward my long-range goal?"

2 Weeks Name a simple one-time activity to get you started.

MY FIVE-YEAR SPIRITUAL GROWTH GOALS
SAMPLE PAGE

5 Years *Finish reading the Bible all the way through.*

3 Years *Finish reading Old Testament. Start reading New Testament.*

1 Year *Read Genesis, Exodus, and Psalms. Then start reading rest of Old Testament.*

6 Months *Read Gospel of John. Memorize John 3:16.*

2 Weeks *Make a checklist of books of the Bible I want to know more about and read up on those books in a study Bible.*

MY FIVE-YEAR SPIRITUAL GROWTH GOALS
My Page

5 Years _____

3 Years _____

1 Year _____

6 Months _____

2 Weeks _____

MY FIVE-YEAR FINANCIAL STABILITY GOALS

HELPS PAGE

5 Years   Create a five-year Financial Stability goal that is important to you. Your goal could relate to assets, income, property, or giving.

3 Years   Ask yourself, "What specific thing will demonstrate that I am coming closer and closer to achieving my Financial Stability goal?"

1 Year   Use this thought starter: "What will I personally commit to accomplish (or stop doing) in the next year to begin developing a financially stable lifestyle?"

6 Months Ask, "What can I be doing six months from now that is directly related to my five-year Financial Stability goal?"

2 Weeks Think of a two-week financial stability activity that doesn't require any other people or finances that you don't yet have.

MY FIVE-YEAR FINANCIAL STABILITY GOALS
SAMPLE PAGE

5 Years   *Put down-payment on a house.*

3 Years   *Save up one half of down-payment for a house.*

1 Year   *Save $1,000. Look for a better-paying job.*

6 Months   *Save $500. Begin tithing to my church.*

2 Weeks   *Ask bank about savings account options. Look at some books on personal finances at my local bookstore or library.*

MY FIVE-YEAR FINANCIAL STABILITY GOALS
MY PAGE

5 Years _____

3 Years _____

1 Year _____

6 Months _____

2 Weeks _____

PARTNERING WITH GOD

God can give you good things despite your current circumstances or environment, but His normal method is to partner with you and others to improve your circumstances and environment as you grow and develop spiritually.

> *"Beloved, I pray that you may prosper in all things and be in health, just as your soul prospers."*—3 John 2

ACCOMPLISHING YOUR GOALS

The good goals that you seek for yourself usually will be easier to accomplish in the company of other believers. Being a loner is not much fun. It's not very productive either.

Who do you know who could help you reach your goals?

Who do you know that *you* could help?

If you want to succeed in any area of life, find a way to serve others.

> *"Whoever desires to become great among you, let him be your servant. And whoever desires to be first among you, let him be your slave—just as the Son of Man did not come to be served, but to serve, and to give His life a ransom for many."*—Matthew 20:26–28

Whether you're a leader or a follower, judge people with fairness and justice, not by their looks or social connections.

Help *them* to have good goals; then good things will happen to you because you are a fair person.

And remember, even if you never become a leader, you can always be fair and stand for what is right.

> *"The LORD does not see as man sees; for man looks at the outward appearance, but the Lord looks at the heart."*—1 Samuel 16:7

Share your goals, dreams, and values
frequently with your friends, your
church family, and your coworkers.

And don't forget to listen to their
goals, dreams, and values.

In other words:

- The lone eagle seldom wins the prize.

- The good you seek for yourself will be found in the company of others.

- The high position to which you aspire will only come when you have brought benefit to others.

- It is when we serve that we are served. That is perhaps the ultimate way in which we partner with God.

*T*homas Edison was in love with electricity. His invention of a reliable light bulb made the rest of the country want electricity in their farms, homes, and offices too.

But Edison didn't succeed on his own. His light-bulb team consisted of more than thirty inventors and engineers. They worked together over many months to develop a bulb that could be easily manufactured and distributed.

It was the benefits of his work—and his partnership with others—that put Edison on the map.

Perhaps in this achievement Edison realized the truth of what Jesus said: "He who seeks to be the master must be the servant of all."

WHAT ABOUT GIVING?

Learning to receive the good that God is trying to bring into your life is critical. Giving God the credit for the good that comes to you is ethical. Sharing that good with others is moral.

Just because God is bringing good things into your life is no reason to act in a selfish manner. Jesus teaches that what you give and do sacrificially for others will be rewarded by God Himself.

> *"When you do a charitable deed, do not let your left hand know what your right hand is doing, that your charitable deed may be in secret; and your Father who sees in secret will Himself reward you."*—Matthew 6:3–4

Your family, your church, and your community need the best of what you can give to them.

Many thousands of people donate to United Way, The Salvation Army, and other groups that help the poor. Usually, those who give seek no rewards, but they are blessed because of their giving.

Those institutions and individuals who are most generous in sharing what they have with others are often those who most frequently experience something good happening to them.

Complete the circle. Be a giver, as well as a receiver, of the good.

> *"But seek first the kingdom of God and His righteousness, and all these things shall be added to you."*—Matthew 6:33

obert Franklin is a noted black social commentator and Christian activist who rose to become the tenth president of Morehouse College in Atlanta.

As a young college student, he was studying while others were partying. His life is a model for those who seek to promote social justice and financial stability for the nation's poor.

In his book *Crisis in the Village*, he challenges some of America's wealthiest churches—and all of us as individuals—to invest more in uplifting the poor and the marginalized in our society.

TRUSTING GOD FOR YOUR GOOD FUTURE

You might sometimes doubt your own abilities, but you should never doubt that God promises you something good.

If you check out Jeremiah 29:11, you'll see that God promises you both a future *and* a hope. That's as good as good gets!

Proverbs 17:22 says, "A merry heart does good, like medicine." So smile as often as you can. After all, something good is trying to happen to you!

DOING THE MOST GOOD

I'm gonna keep on striving
To be the best that I can,
To achieve all my dreams,
From way back when.

I was just a young lad
Giving my best attempt,
To make it in life
Is what I always dreamt.

In order to be something
You must first believe.
That's the main ingredient
For anyone to achieve.

—Mark Jackson

Quoted on a sign in a new car dealership (title added)

A Final Thought

The most popular Scripture verse for new Christians to memorize is Philippians 4:13, "I can do all things through Christ who strengthens me." Make it yours and expect God's goodness to come your way, starting today!

*M*ajor John R. Cheydleur, Ph.D., is a long-service officer in The Salvation Army. The Salvation Army's motto is "Heart to God, hand to man." Its theology and practice assert that God cares about the rich, the poor, and the in-between, and that He has designed us to find our highest fulfillment when we cooperate with His plan for our lives.

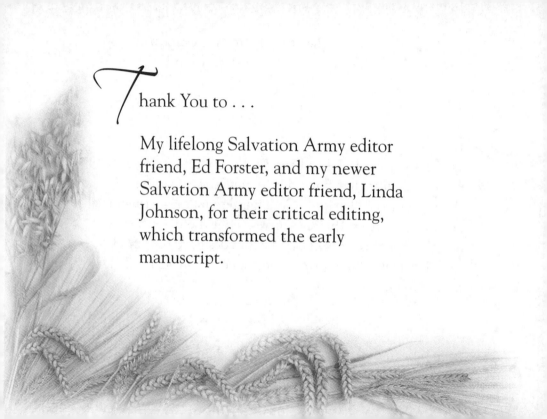

*T*hank You to . . .

My lifelong Salvation Army editor friend, Ed Forster, and my newer Salvation Army editor friend, Linda Johnson, for their critical editing, which transformed the early manuscript.

$\mathcal{T}$hank You to . . .

Beth Ryan and Randy Elliot
"adopted" the project for Thomas
Nelson Publishers. They brought it
to life through their talented editorial
and book production resources.
Beth's daughter Katie contributed the
"Godcidence" idea.

*T*hank You to . . .

Daisy Sanchez who faithfully typed
and retyped seemingly endless
changes in the manuscript, all with a
cheerful and positive spirit.

Commissioners Larry and Nancy
Moretz of The Salvation Army.
Their support has been invaluable.